EMMANUEL JOSEPH

From Wall Street to the World Stage, How Billionaires Influence Nations and Economies

Copyright © 2025 by Emmanuel Joseph

All rights reserved. No part of this publication may be reproduced, stored or transmitted in any form or by any means, electronic, mechanical, photocopying, recording, scanning, or otherwise without written permission from the publisher. It is illegal to copy this book, post it to a website, or distribute it by any other means without permission.

First edition

This book was professionally typeset on Reedsy. Find out more at reedsy.com

Contents

1. Chapter 1: The Rise of the Modern Billionaire — 1
2. Chapter 2: Economic Powerhouses — 3
3. Chapter 3: Political Influence — 5
4. Chapter 4: Globalization and Capital Flows — 7
5. Chapter 5: Technology and Innovation — 9
6. Chapter 6: Media Moguls and Public Perception — 11
7. Chapter 7: Philanthropy and Social Responsibility — 13
8. Chapter 8: Environmental Impact and Sustainability — 15
9. Chapter 9: Income Inequality and Social Disparities — 17
10. Chapter 10: The Dark Side of Wealth — 19
11. Chapter 11: Cultural and Artistic Patronage — 21
12. Chapter 12: The Future of Work — 23
13. Chapter 13: Education and Knowledge Economy — 25
14. Chapter 14: Health and Biotechnology — 27
15. Chapter 15: Space Exploration and Beyond — 29
16. Chapter 16: The Role of Family and Succession — 31
17. Chapter 17: The Ethical Imperative — 33

1

Chapter 1: The Rise of the Modern Billionaire

In the 21st century, the phenomenon of the modern billionaire has become a defining feature of global wealth distribution. Technological advancements, globalization, and innovative business models have paved the way for individuals to accumulate unprecedented fortunes. Historically, wealth was concentrated among royalty and aristocrats, but today, billionaires often emerge from humble beginnings, driven by entrepreneurial spirit and strategic vision. Figures like Bill Gates, Jeff Bezos, and Elon Musk epitomize this new wave of wealth, reshaping industries and setting new benchmarks for success.

These billionaires are not merely passive beneficiaries of economic growth; they are active architects of their fortunes. Through strategic investments, visionary leadership, and a keen understanding of market dynamics, they have built empires that transcend national boundaries. Their companies, often at the forefront of technological innovation, have disrupted traditional industries and created new markets. The influence of these billionaires extends far beyond their balance sheets, as they shape the global economic landscape and set trends that others strive to follow.

The meteoric rise of modern billionaires is also a testament to the power of technology. The digital revolution has created opportunities for rapid wealth accumulation, with tech entrepreneurs leading the charge. Companies like Amazon, Microsoft, and Tesla have not only revolutionized their respective fields but have also created vast ecosystems of innovation and economic activity. The ability to leverage data, software, and digital platforms has enabled these billionaires to achieve scale and efficiency that were previously unimaginable.

As we examine the rise of modern billionaires, it is essential to consider the broader implications of their influence. While their success stories inspire admiration and aspiration, they also raise important questions about wealth inequality, economic power, and social responsibility. The concentration of wealth among a select few individuals has far-reaching consequences for society, shaping public policy, political agendas, and cultural narratives. Understanding the rise of modern billionaires is not just about celebrating their achievements, but also about critically examining the impact of their wealth on the world.

2

Chapter 2: Economic Powerhouses

Billionaires wield immense economic power that can surpass the GDP of small nations. Their investment strategies and business ventures have far-reaching impacts on industries and economies around the world. Through strategic acquisitions, mergers, and market expansion, they create economic ecosystems that drive growth and innovation. This chapter delves into the ways billionaires leverage their wealth to shape the economic landscape.

Investment decisions made by billionaires can influence entire markets. Their financial backing can propel startups into industry giants or save struggling companies from bankruptcy. By injecting capital into various sectors, they foster economic dynamism and job creation. Moreover, their involvement in venture capital and private equity enables them to identify and nurture promising enterprises, further solidifying their economic clout.

Philanthropic endeavors also play a significant role in their economic influence. By establishing foundations and funding social initiatives, billionaires address pressing global issues such as poverty, education, and healthcare. These philanthropic efforts not only create positive social impact but also enhance their public image and legacy. However, it is essential to critically examine the effectiveness and motivations behind such charitable activities, as they may also serve to reinforce their power and control.

The economic power of billionaires extends beyond national borders, making them key players in the global economy. Through international investments and multinational enterprises, they shape trade relations, influence regulatory frameworks, and drive economic policies. Their ability to navigate and capitalize on global market trends positions them as formidable economic powerhouses, with the potential to reshape economies on a grand scale.

3

Chapter 3: Political Influence

The political influence of billionaires is a topic of significant interest and concern. Through lobbying, campaign contributions, and strategic alliances, they can sway policy decisions and legislative outcomes. This chapter examines the intricate web of connections between wealth and politics, exploring how billionaires shape governance and public policy.

Lobbying efforts by billionaires and their corporations are a powerful tool for influencing political agendas. By funding think tanks, advocacy groups, and political campaigns, they can promote policies that align with their business interests. This financial support often grants them access to key decision-makers, allowing them to shape legislation in ways that benefit their enterprises.

Campaign contributions are another avenue through which billionaires exert political influence. By donating to political candidates and parties, they gain favor and influence over policy decisions. This practice raises concerns about the integrity of democratic processes, as it can lead to a disproportionate representation of wealthy interests at the expense of the broader population.

Strategic alliances between billionaires and political figures further amplify their influence. By leveraging their wealth and networks, they can forge partnerships that advance their mutual interests. These alliances often extend to the international stage, where billionaires collaborate with foreign governments and institutions to shape global policies and agendas.

The political influence of billionaires raises important questions about the balance of power in democratic societies. While their contributions can drive positive change and innovation, they also pose risks to transparency, accountability, and equity. Understanding the complex interplay between wealth and politics is essential for addressing these challenges and ensuring a fair and just political system.

4

Chapter 4: Globalization and Capital Flows

Globalization has facilitated the flow of capital across borders, allowing billionaires to expand their influence internationally. This chapter explores the mechanisms through which they invest in foreign markets and establish multinational enterprises, as well as the regulatory challenges and ethical considerations associated with their global reach.

The ability to move capital freely across borders has opened up new opportunities for billionaires to invest in diverse markets. By acquiring assets, forming joint ventures, and establishing subsidiaries in foreign countries, they can tap into emerging economies and maximize returns on investment. This global expansion not only drives economic growth but also enhances their strategic positioning in the global market.

However, the international activities of billionaires are not without challenges. Navigating complex regulatory environments, managing cross-cultural differences, and mitigating geopolitical risks are critical aspects of their global operations. Furthermore, their influence on local economies can raise ethical concerns, particularly when it comes to labor practices, environmental impact, and cultural preservation.

The role of billionaires in shaping globalization extends beyond economic transactions. Through their involvement in international organizations, trade agreements, and diplomatic efforts, they can influence global policies and standards. This chapter examines the ways in which billionaires leverage their wealth and networks to shape the global economic landscape and drive the agenda for international cooperation.

As we consider the impact of globalization on the influence of billionaires, it is essential to reflect on the broader implications for society. While their investments can bring economic benefits and development opportunities, they also raise questions about inequality, sovereignty, and ethical responsibility. Understanding the dynamics of globalization and capital flows is crucial for navigating the complexities of the modern global economy.

5

Chapter 5: Technology and Innovation

Technological innovation is a key driver of wealth creation for many billionaires. This chapter highlights the groundbreaking inventions and advancements pioneered by these individuals, exploring the ecosystems that foster innovation and the role billionaires play in driving technological progress.

The digital revolution has been a major catalyst for the rise of modern billionaires. Tech entrepreneurs like Steve Jobs, Mark Zuckerberg, and Jack Ma have leveraged the power of technology to create transformative products and services that have reshaped industries and consumer behaviors. By harnessing the potential of digital platforms, data analytics, and artificial intelligence, they have revolutionized the way we live and work.

Innovation ecosystems, such as Silicon Valley, play a crucial role in fostering technological advancements. These ecosystems provide the infrastructure, talent, and resources necessary for startups and established companies to thrive. Billionaires often act as mentors, investors, and thought leaders within these ecosystems, nurturing the next generation of innovators and driving the continuous evolution of technology.

The role of billionaires in driving technological progress extends beyond their entrepreneurial endeavors. Through investments in research and development, they contribute to scientific breakthroughs and technological advancements. Their support for universities, research institutions, and innovation hubs accelerates the pace of discovery and commercialization, pushing the boundaries of what is possible.

While technological innovation brings numerous benefits, it also poses challenges and ethical considerations. The rapid pace of change can lead to disruptions in labor markets, privacy concerns, and societal inequalities. This chapter explores the responsibilities of billionaires in addressing these challenges and ensuring that technological progress is inclusive and beneficial for all.

6

Chapter 6: Media Moguls and Public Perception

The media industry is a powerful tool for shaping public opinion, and many billionaires have significant stakes in major media outlets. By controlling narratives and influencing public discourse, they wield substantial power over how information is disseminated and perceived. This chapter investigates the ways in which billionaires leverage their media ownership to impact society and culture.

Media ownership allows billionaires to shape the news agenda and frame issues in ways that align with their interests and perspectives. Through newspapers, television networks, and digital platforms, they can influence public opinion on political, economic, and social matters. By controlling the flow of information, they have the ability to sway public perception and mold societal norms.

The concentration of media ownership among billionaires raises important questions about media diversity and independence. When a few wealthy individuals dominate the media landscape, there is a risk of biased reporting and a lack of diverse viewpoints. This chapter explores the implications of media consolidation and the potential threats to journalistic integrity and democratic discourse.

Beyond traditional media, billionaires also invest in emerging digital platforms and social media networks. These platforms have become critical channels for news consumption and communication, amplifying the reach and impact of billionaire influence. By leveraging their investments in technology and media, billionaires can shape the digital public sphere and drive the conversation on global issues.

The influence of media moguls on public perception highlights the importance of media literacy and critical thinking. As consumers of information, it is essential to be aware of the potential biases and motivations behind the news we consume. By fostering media literacy, we can better navigate the complex media landscape and make informed decisions in an era of billionaire-dominated media.

7

Chapter 7: Philanthropy and Social Responsibility

Philanthropy is often seen as a way for billionaires to give back to society and address pressing global issues. This chapter explores the motivations behind their charitable contributions and the impact of their philanthropic initiatives, while also discussing the criticism and skepticism surrounding billionaire philanthropy.

Billionaire philanthropists establish foundations and fund social programs to tackle challenges such as poverty, education, healthcare, and environmental sustainability. Their financial resources enable them to support large-scale projects and initiatives that can create meaningful change. By directing their wealth towards philanthropy, they can leave a positive legacy and make a difference in the lives of many.

However, the motivations behind billionaire philanthropy are complex and multifaceted. While some are driven by genuine altruism and a desire to make a positive impact, others may use philanthropy as a means to enhance their public image and mitigate criticism. This chapter examines the various factors that influence billionaire philanthropy and the potential for conflicts of interest.

Critics argue that billionaire philanthropy can perpetuate existing power dynamics and undermine democratic processes. When wealthy individuals control significant philanthropic resources, they can shape social agendas and priorities in ways that align with their personal interests. This chapter explores the ethical considerations and potential pitfalls of billionaire-driven philanthropy.

Despite the criticisms, billionaire philanthropy has the potential to address systemic issues and create lasting social change. By focusing on evidence-based strategies and collaborating with stakeholders, philanthropists can maximize the impact of their contributions. This chapter highlights successful examples of billionaire philanthropy and the lessons learned from their efforts to create a more just and equitable world.

8

Chapter 8: Environmental Impact and Sustainability

Billionaires are increasingly involved in environmental conservation and sustainability efforts. This chapter examines their role in tackling climate change, promoting renewable energy, and supporting green technologies, as well as the potential conflicts of interest that arise when their business interests clash with environmental goals.

Climate change is one of the most pressing global challenges, and billionaires have the financial resources and influence to drive significant progress in addressing it. Through investments in renewable energy, electric vehicles, and sustainable agriculture, they can support the transition to a low-carbon economy. This chapter explores the contributions of billionaire environmentalists and their impact on sustainability.

Billionaires also fund research and innovation in green technologies, aiming to develop solutions that can mitigate environmental harm and promote sustainability. By supporting startups and initiatives focused on clean energy, circular economy, and conservation, they can accelerate the adoption of sustainable practices. This chapter highlights the role of billionaires in fostering environmental innovation.

However, the environmental impact of billionaires is not without controversy. Some critics argue that their business practices and investments in industries such as fossil fuels, mining, and manufacturing contribute to environmental degradation. This chapter examines the potential conflicts of interest and the ethical dilemmas that arise when billionaires' economic activities clash with their sustainability goals.

The involvement of billionaires in environmental conservation also raises questions about accountability and transparency. While their contributions can drive positive change, it is essential to ensure that their efforts are aligned with scientific evidence and ethical standards. This chapter discusses the importance of holding billionaires accountable for their environmental impact and promoting responsible stewardship of the planet.

9

Chapter 9: Income Inequality and Social Disparities

The concentration of wealth among billionaires contributes to growing income inequality and social disparities. This chapter delves into the societal consequences of such disparities, including access to education, healthcare, and opportunities, and explores potential solutions to bridge the gap.

Income inequality has far-reaching implications for social cohesion and economic stability. When wealth is concentrated in the hands of a few, it can lead to disparities in access to essential services and opportunities. This chapter examines the impact of billionaire wealth on education, healthcare, housing, and social mobility, highlighting the challenges faced by marginalized communities.

The role of billionaires in perpetuating or addressing income inequality is a topic of significant debate. While some argue that their investments and philanthropic efforts can create opportunities and drive economic growth, others contend that their wealth concentration exacerbates social disparities. This chapter explores the different perspectives on the relationship between billionaires and income inequality.

Addressing income inequality requires a multifaceted approach that includes policy interventions, social programs, and economic reforms. This chapter examines potential solutions such as progressive taxation, universal basic income, affordable housing initiatives, and access to quality education and healthcare. By exploring these strategies, we can envision a more equitable and inclusive society.

The involvement of billionaires in efforts to address income inequality also raises important ethical and philosophical questions. How can we ensure that their contributions are genuinely aimed at reducing disparities rather than reinforcing their power? This chapter discusses the importance of transparency, accountability, and inclusive decision-making in tackling income inequality and promoting social justice.

10

Chapter 10: The Dark Side of Wealth

With great wealth often comes great controversy. This chapter sheds light on the darker aspects of billionaire influence, including tax avoidance, monopolistic practices, and exploitation of labor. By examining these issues, we uncover the ethical dilemmas and legal challenges that arise from extreme wealth concentration.

Tax avoidance is a common practice among billionaires, allowing them to minimize their tax liabilities through legal loopholes and offshore accounts. While these strategies may be within the bounds of the law, they raise questions about fairness and equity. This chapter explores the methods used by billionaires to reduce their tax burden and the impact on public finances and social welfare programs.

Monopolistic practices are another contentious aspect of billionaire influence. By acquiring competitors, controlling supply chains, and leveraging market power, billionaires can stifle competition and create barriers to entry for new businesses. This chapter examines the implications of monopolies on innovation, consumer choice, and market dynamics. We also consider the role of antitrust regulations in curbing monopolistic behavior.

The exploitation of labor is a significant ethical concern associated with billionaire wealth. In pursuit of profit, some billionaires have been accused of underpaying workers, providing poor working conditions, and engaging in exploitative labor practices. This chapter delves into the labor issues faced by workers in industries dominated by billionaire-owned companies, highlighting the need for fair labor standards and corporate accountability.

The dark side of wealth also extends to the environmental and social impact of billionaires' business activities. From environmental degradation to human rights violations, the pursuit of profit can sometimes come at a high cost. This chapter explores the ethical dilemmas and legal challenges associated with billionaire influence, emphasizing the importance of responsible and sustainable business practices.

11

Chapter 11: Cultural and Artistic Patronage

Billionaires have long been patrons of the arts and culture, supporting museums, galleries, and cultural institutions. This chapter explores the ways in which their patronage shapes artistic expression and cultural heritage, as well as the potential biases and power dynamics that arise when art is influenced by wealthy benefactors.

Cultural patronage allows billionaires to leave a lasting impact on the arts and humanities. By funding museums, theaters, and art galleries, they can support the preservation and promotion of cultural heritage. This chapter examines the motivations behind billionaire patronage and the ways in which their contributions enhance the cultural landscape.

However, the influence of wealthy benefactors on the arts is not without controversy. When billionaires fund cultural institutions, they may exert control over artistic decisions, curatorial practices, and institutional policies. This chapter explores the potential biases and power dynamics that arise when art is influenced by the interests and preferences of wealthy patrons.

The impact of billionaire patronage on cultural heritage extends beyond financial support. By commissioning artworks, sponsoring exhibitions, and funding cultural programs, billionaires can shape the narratives and themes that define artistic expression. This chapter examines the ways in which their patronage influences the creation and interpretation of art, as well as the implications for cultural diversity and representation.

While billionaire patronage can bring significant benefits to the arts, it also raises important ethical questions. How can we ensure that cultural institutions remain independent and inclusive? This chapter discusses the need for transparency, accountability, and diverse funding sources to maintain the integrity and vitality of the arts.

12

Chapter 12: The Future of Work

The rise of automation and artificial intelligence, driven by investments from billionaires, is transforming the future of work. This chapter investigates the implications of technological disruption on employment, labor markets, and job creation, and considers potential solutions to mitigate the negative effects of automation.

Automation and artificial intelligence are reshaping industries and redefining the nature of work. Billionaires at the forefront of technological innovation are investing heavily in these technologies, driving advancements that enhance efficiency and productivity. This chapter explores the ways in which automation is transforming various sectors, from manufacturing to healthcare, and the impact on the workforce.

The displacement of jobs due to automation is a significant concern. As machines and algorithms take over routine and repetitive tasks, workers in certain industries face the risk of unemployment and underemployment. This chapter examines the challenges posed by technological disruption and the need for reskilling and upskilling programs to help workers adapt to the changing labor market.

The future of work also raises questions about the quality and nature of employment. While automation can create new opportunities and job categories, it may also lead to increased precarity and inequality. This chapter explores the implications of gig economy platforms, remote work, and digital labor, highlighting the need for policies that ensure fair labor standards and social protection.

Addressing the challenges of the future of work requires collaboration between stakeholders, including governments, businesses, and workers. This chapter discusses potential solutions, such as social safety nets, lifelong learning initiatives, and inclusive economic policies, to mitigate the negative effects of automation and create a more equitable and sustainable future of work.

13

Chapter 13: Education and Knowledge Economy

Education is a key area where billionaires exert significant influence. This chapter examines their investments in educational institutions, research initiatives, and scholarship programs, exploring the impact of their contributions on the knowledge economy and future generations.

Billionaire investments in education can have a transformative impact on academic institutions and research endeavors. By funding universities, research centers, and scholarship programs, they support the advancement of knowledge and the development of human capital. This chapter highlights the ways in which billionaires contribute to the education sector and the potential benefits of their involvement.

The role of billionaires in shaping the knowledge economy extends beyond financial support. Through strategic partnerships and collaborations, they can drive innovation and create opportunities for interdisciplinary research and development. This chapter explores the impact of billionaire-backed initiatives on scientific discovery, technological advancement, and economic growth.

However, the influence of billionaires on education also raises concerns about access, equity, and academic independence. When wealthy individuals fund educational institutions, there is a risk of prioritizing certain fields of study or research agendas that align with their interests. This chapter examines the potential biases and power dynamics that arise from billionaire involvement in education and the implications for academic freedom and diversity.

Ensuring that education remains accessible and inclusive is a critical challenge in the face of growing wealth concentration. This chapter discusses the importance of equitable funding models, transparent governance, and inclusive policies to ensure that billionaire contributions to education benefit all students and researchers. By addressing these challenges, we can harness the potential of the knowledge economy to create a more just and prosperous society.

14

Chapter 14: Health and Biotechnology

Billionaires are at the forefront of advancements in health and biotechnology, funding research and development in these fields. This chapter explores their contributions to medical breakthroughs, drug development, and healthcare innovation, as well as the ethical considerations and potential risks associated with their involvement in the health sector.

The financial resources of billionaires allow them to support cutting-edge research and development in health and biotechnology. By funding academic institutions, research centers, and biotech startups, they accelerate the discovery of new treatments and medical technologies. This chapter highlights the impact of billionaire-backed initiatives on medical breakthroughs, such as gene editing, personalized medicine, and regenerative therapies.

Drug development is a key area where billionaires have made significant contributions. Through investments in pharmaceutical companies and biotech firms, they support the development of new drugs and therapies that can address unmet medical needs. This chapter examines the role of billionaires in advancing drug discovery and the potential benefits for patients and healthcare systems.

Healthcare innovation is another important aspect of billionaire influence in the health sector. By funding initiatives focused on digital health, telemedicine, and health data analytics, they drive the adoption of new technologies that can improve patient outcomes and enhance healthcare delivery. This chapter explores the ways in which billionaires are transforming healthcare through innovation and technology.

However, the involvement of billionaires in health and biotechnology also raises ethical considerations and potential risks. Issues such as access to new treatments, data privacy, and the commercialization of scientific research are critical areas of concern. This chapter discusses the ethical dilemmas and regulatory challenges associated with billionaire influence in the health sector and the importance of ensuring that medical advancements benefit all members of society.

15

Chapter 15: Space Exploration and Beyond

Space exploration has captured the imagination of billionaires, leading to significant investments in private space ventures. This chapter delves into the ambitions and achievements of billionaire space explorers, exploring the potential benefits and challenges of privatized space exploration and its implications for humanity's future.

Billionaire entrepreneurs such as Elon Musk, Jeff Bezos, and Richard Branson have made headlines with their ambitious space ventures. By founding companies like SpaceX, Blue Origin, and Virgin Galactic, they have pushed the boundaries of space exploration and commercial space travel. This chapter highlights the achievements of these space pioneers and their contributions to the aerospace industry.

Private space ventures have the potential to drive innovation and reduce the cost of space exploration. By developing reusable rockets, advanced propulsion systems, and cutting-edge spacecraft, billionaire-funded companies are making space more accessible and opening up new possibilities for scientific research and commercial activities. This chapter explores the technological advancements and economic opportunities created by privatized space exploration.

However, the involvement of billionaires in space exploration also raises important questions about the commercialization and governance of space. Issues such as space debris, resource exploitation, and the potential for conflict in space require careful consideration and international cooperation. This chapter examines the ethical and regulatory challenges associated with private space ventures and the need for a balanced approach to space exploration.

The ambitions of billionaire space explorers extend beyond Earth's orbit, with visions of colonizing Mars, establishing lunar bases, and developing space tourism. While these aspirations inspire excitement and optimism, they also pose significant technical, financial, and ethical challenges. This chapter discusses the long-term implications of billionaire-driven space exploration and the potential for humanity to become a multi-planetary species.

16

Chapter 16: The Role of Family and Succession

Many billionaires are concerned with preserving their wealth and legacy for future generations. This chapter examines the role of family dynamics, succession planning, and intergenerational wealth transfer, exploring the sustainability of billionaire influence over time.

Family dynamics play a crucial role in the management and preservation of billionaire wealth. Many billionaires involve their family members in their business ventures and philanthropic activities, creating a legacy that extends beyond their own lifetime. This chapter explores the ways in which billionaire families manage their wealth and the challenges they face in maintaining unity and cohesion.

Succession planning is a critical aspect of preserving billionaire wealth and influence. Ensuring a smooth transition of leadership and ownership requires careful planning and consideration of various factors, such as the abilities and aspirations of potential successors, tax implications, and legal requirements. This chapter examines the strategies employed by billionaire families to navigate succession planning and secure their legacy.

Intergenerational wealth transfer is another important consideration for billionaire families. By establishing trusts, foundations, and family offices, they can manage the distribution of wealth across generations and support philanthropic initiatives. This chapter explores the mechanisms of intergenerational wealth transfer and the potential benefits and challenges associated with preserving wealth over the long term.

The sustainability of billionaire influence over time depends on various factors, including the ability to adapt to changing economic and social conditions, the effectiveness of succession planning, and the commitment to responsible stewardship. This chapter discusses the importance of resilience, innovation, and ethical leadership in ensuring the continued impact of billionaire families on society and the economy.

17

Chapter 17: The Ethical Imperative

The influence of billionaires on nations and economies raises important ethical questions. This chapter concludes the book by exploring the moral responsibilities of the ultra-wealthy, discussing the need for accountability, transparency, and a commitment to the greater good, and envisioning a more equitable and just future.

The concentration of wealth and power among billionaires necessitates a discussion of their ethical responsibilities. As influential actors in the global economy, they have the potential to drive positive change but also bear the responsibility to act in the best interests of society. This chapter examines the moral imperatives for billionaires to prioritize social justice, environmental sustainability, and economic equity.

Accountability and transparency are essential components of ethical leadership. Billionaires must be held accountable for their actions and decisions, ensuring that their influence is exercised responsibly and in accordance with ethical standards. This chapter explores the mechanisms for promoting accountability and transparency, such as regulatory frameworks, independent oversight, and public scrutiny.

A commitment to the greater good is fundamental to addressing the challenges and opportunities associated with billionaire influence. By leveraging their resources and networks for the benefit of society, billionaires can contribute to solutions for pressing global issues such as poverty, climate change, and inequality. This chapter highlights examples of ethical leadership and the potential for billionaire-driven initiatives to create positive social impact.

Envisioning a more equitable and just future requires a collaborative effort among billionaires, policymakers, and civil society. By promoting inclusive economic policies, fostering innovation, and supporting social justice initiatives, we can create a world where the benefits of wealth and progress are shared more broadly. This chapter concludes the book by outlining a vision for a future in which billionaire influence is harnessed for the greater good, contributing to a more just and prosperous society.

From Wall Street to the World Stage: How Billionaires Influence Nations and Economies takes readers on a fascinating journey into the world of modern billionaires and their profound impact on global economies and societies. This insightful book explores the origins and rise of billionaires, highlighting their remarkable entrepreneurial journeys and the technological advancements that have enabled their unprecedented wealth accumulation.

Through a comprehensive analysis, the book delves into the vast economic influence wielded by billionaires, examining their investment strategies, business ventures, and philanthropic endeavors. It sheds light on their ability to shape industries, drive innovation, and create economic ecosystems that generate significant employment and growth.

The political influence of billionaires is also scrutinized, revealing the ways in which they lobby, fund campaigns, and form strategic alliances to sway policy decisions and legislative outcomes. The book uncovers the intricate web of connections between wealth and politics, raising critical questions about the balance of power in democratic societies.

Globalization and technological innovation are central themes, as the book explores how billionaires invest in foreign markets, establish multinational enterprises, and drive technological progress. The impact of their media ownership on public perception, their philanthropic initiatives, and their contributions to environmental sustainability are thoroughly examined, providing a nuanced understanding of their multifaceted influence.

The book does not shy away from addressing the ethical dilemmas and controversies surrounding billionaires. It explores issues such as tax avoidance, monopolistic practices, labor exploitation, and the potential biases in cultural and artistic patronage. Additionally, it discusses the societal consequences of income inequality and the responsibilities of billionaires to address these disparities.

From the future of work shaped by automation and artificial intelligence to the ambitious ventures in space exploration, the book provides a holistic view of how billionaires are transforming the world. It concludes by examining the moral imperatives and ethical responsibilities of the ultra-wealthy, envisioning a more equitable and just future where billionaire influence is harnessed for the greater good.

From Wall Street to the World Stage is a thought-provoking and comprehensive exploration of the ways in which billionaires shape nations and economies, offering readers a deeper understanding of their impact on the world and the ethical considerations that accompany their immense wealth and power.

www.ingramcontent.com/pod-product-compliance
Lightning Source LLC
LaVergne TN
LVHW020458080526
838202LV00057B/6018